CHICAGO

CHICAGO

PHOTOGRAPHS BY **SANTI VISALLI**

FOREWORD BY BILL KURTIS

RIZZOLI
NEW YORK

The thoughts on Chicago that appear in this book are those of the persons cited below. Numbers in parentheses indicate pages on which the contributions appear.

First published in the United States of America in 1987 by
RIZZOLI INTERNATIONAL PUBLICATIONS, INC.
300 Park Avenue South, New York, NY 10010

Library of Congress Cataloging-in-Publication Data

Visalli, Santi.
  Chicago.
    1. Chicago (Ill.)—Description—1981–1987—Views.
2. Architecture—Illinois—Chicago—Pictorial works.
I. Title.
F548.37.V57 1987   779′.9977311043   87-45391
ISBN 0-8478-0842-4

Designed by Gilda Hannah
Set in type by David Seham Associates, Metuchen, N.J.
Printed and bound by Toppan Printing Co., Japan

Reprinted in 1989

To Gayla,
Ivon, and Loren

ACKNOWLEDGMENTS

This book would never have been possible without the legions of Chicagoans who pointed me in the right direction and smoothed the path. Among them were Mrs. Marilyn Clancy of the Chicago Tourism Council and her staff, who arranged numerous introductions; Jack Star, who directec me to a rare picture; Mrs. Cindy Mitchell of the Friends of the Parks; architect Peter Roesch, who showed me not a few of the architectural gems of Chicago and filled me in on the city's great architectural history; his lovely wife Biba, who opened many doors for me; Henry Goldstein, General Manager of the Mayfair Regent Hotel, who provided me with a home away from home; and an army of security guards who led me to countless windy rooftops.

Thank you also to the Chicago Film Office, photographer David Maenza, Claudette Mostyn of the Image Bank, and my two assistants, Jill Barancik of Chicago and Federico Antonucci, an Italian student from Parma.Federico, because of his patience and ability to improvise, turned out to be one of the best assistants I've ever had (even at 6:00 A.M., with the temperature at -23° F, he kept his smile and his cool).

I would like to thank my publisher, Gianfranco Monacelli, for entrusting me with the creation of this book; my editors, Lauren Shakely and Solveig Williams, for the encouraging words they so generously dispensed each time I returned from Chicago; and my designer, Gilda Hannah, who never compromised on the quality of a photograph—declaring: "I don't care if it *is* important, it has to be beautiful."

A special thank you goes to Bill Kurtis for accompanying me on several shoots, for sharing with me his great love of Chicago, and above all for honoring me with his foreword to this book.

Santi Visalli

FOREWORD

BILL KURTIS

There's a *new* Chicago rising. It's bursting through old buildings in the Loop to create sparkling glass canyons. It's sprouting towers of poured concrete in empty railroad yards and crawling into skeletons of aging factories to replace the blue collars with white. Even the early sun seems to dance lightly over the sharp new angles in its skyline. And its sound—the sound that hums from the neighborhoods and ball parks and scaffolds—is the sound of renewal.

It's not the first time Chicago has changed. Every great city is always growing and dying at the same time: "Building, breaking, rebuilding," as Carl Sandburg described Chicago in 1916. He was the child of immigrant parents who came out of the prairie to behold this giant by the Lake with a sense of wonder. Skyscrapers that others would take for granted and disparage, he exalted. Where they would see another overgrown industrial city, Sandburg saw "a tall bold slugger set vivid against the little soft cities."

Sometimes it takes a visitor to show us the change. Someone who can see it with fresh eyes. Someone like Santi Visalli. His photographs depict a city we knew was there but had not seen so clearly before. Armed with his cameras, this photo journalist arrived, as others have, anxious to record the monuments of Louis Sullivan, Frank Lloyd Wright, and Ludwig Mies van der Rohe. But he was transfixed by the works of a *new* generation of the Chicago School of Architecture.

In the short span of two decades, the city has added a special meaning to its own invention—the skyscraper—with a building that reaches higher than any other in the world and, in its shadow, a translucent cavern where government workers cluster on open ledges like ancient cave dwellers seeking shelter from winter storms. The combination of glass and steel is so striking in its vision of the future that we are thankful for Visalli's photographs—almost afraid that, like Brigadoon, the structures will vanish suddenly, only to rise again in another hundred years from an obscure onion patch in the tall grass prairie of America's middle belt.

The fear may not be totally unfounded. Ironically, the *new* Chicago has taken almost exactly that long to materialize.

It started with a fire. Whether it really began in Mrs. O'Leary's barn doesn't seem to matter now, but we do know she was milking her cow by the light of a kerosene lantern. Her barn was crowded among frame buildings constructed almost entirely of wood. The cow could easily have kicked the lamp into the dry straw to provide the ignition for a firestorm that swept over 15,768 buildings and killed 300 men, women, and children. The fire began October 8, 1871, and when it finally burned itself out, Chicago's claim to being a city was reduced to ghostly images of broken-masonry walls standing above smoking ashes.

Chicagoans measure time from the Great Fire. In countless ways, they still live with decisions made in the days that followed the city's greatest crisis. Within a month, the city elected an extremely able mayor, Joseph Medill, publisher of the *Chicago Tribune*. In his inaugural address, he set the course for strong architectural development by discouraging paper and tar roofs, urging instead "materials as incombustible as brick, stone, iron, or slate."

The city's cultural commitment might be traced to the outpouring of sympathy from thousands of readers around the world who sent books to restock the city's library. Their gifts were placed in an empty water tank above the temporary City Hall. Because it was a favorite pigeon roost, its name "The Rookery" would survive each new building erected on the site. Three days after the fire, the directors of the Chicago Board of Trade resolved to build "the most costly and ornamental structure of its kind in the world," at Jackson and LaSalle streets, anchoring a financial box canyon within the Loop and establishing a thriving trading community that would be growing long after Chicago ceased to be the Hog Butcher for the World. And even before the embers of the Great Fire were cool, Marshall Field reopened for business in the stables of the streetcar company.

So it began. As if a lightning stroke had cleansed the ancient prairie, new shapes quickly sprouted from Chicago's ashes. Brick cottages replaced the wooden-frame shacks. Ornate marble was shaped to the front of granite and sandstone mansions along European boulevards. The city seemed to be rushing to catch up with the rest of the nation, afraid it would miss the expansion into the West. But when it paused long enough to catch its breath, Chicago found itself in the middle of everything, at the head of navigation of the Great Lakes, at the center of the nation's richest coal fields, in the heart of the Mississippi Valley farmlands, at the hub of the nation's railroads.

"Even on a trip to the pearly gates," they would say, "you have to change trains in Chicago."

At the end of twenty years, this sweating, stormy frontier settlement had become all of Sandburg's metaphors: "Hog Butcher for the World, Tool Maker, Stacker of Wheat, Player with Railroads and the Nation's Freight Handler." Chicago had pulled off one of the greatest recoveries of all time and now wanted to brag about it.

On the occasion of the four-hundredth anniversary of the landing of Columbus in America, this rural upstart invited Paris, London, Rome, Tokyo, Berlin, Vienna, Peking—the centers of art, science, royalty, and wealth of the world—to help celebrate. Despite this breathtaking audacity, the World's Columbian Exposition of 1893 evolved into an unparalleled convocation. It came at the height of what artists, scientists, architects, and industrialists believed was an American Renaissance. And it took only one look at the enormous exhibition halls of the "White City," patterned on the world's great architecture, to confirm the sense that America was the legitimate heir to Italy's sixteenth-century accomplishments. When Daniel Burnham, Chief of Construction of the Exposition, later unveiled his Plan of Chicago, the future seemed clear: Chicago would be one of the world's great cities.

Almost a hundred years later, Burnham's Plan is world famous. His fingerprints can be found on the parks, streets, and grand boulevards of Chicago, providing a framework inside which the city has evolved. Santi Visalli's photographs measure that evolution from the windowless shell of the once-prosperous residence hotel of Al Capone to award-winning skyscrapers in another section of town. Whole neighborhoods have disappeared as others explode with new forms. And some never seem to change, as if protected by an unseen guardian.

When Visalli found such architectural giants of Chicago's past as the Adler and Sullivan Auditorium Building still competing for attention with the gaudy newcomers to the Loop, it was as if Daniel Burnham were there, his presence lingering over the city like a Lake Michigan fog on a cold morning. And when Visalli captured a Lake inferno on the verge of consuming the Adler Planetarium, it was like seeing Burnham's passion made visible as his city rose in the dawn.

This city by the Lake can have that effect on you. And it can change its moods with the light. Theodore Dreiser preferred the Chicago evening, "that mystic period between the glare and gloom of the world when life is changing from one sphere or condition to another." Nelson Algren remembered the "nights when the blood-red neon of the tavern legends tether the arc-lamps to all the puddles left from last night's rain, somewhere between the bright carnival of the boulevards and the dark girders of the El."

Algren lived on Chicago's Wild Side, which has changed least of any part of the city. Whiskey has lost its bootleg attraction but is still king of the night, challenged only by cocaine as the sinner's quickest poison.

Guitars and harmonicas that once poured their sounds out the doors of gin mills and apartments to pay the rent today are amplified and heard around the world. They are changing the pulse of the city from the staccato of Capone's machine gun to the pounding beat of Chicago Blues. But violence still staggers mindlessly down the alleys. In the slums, you can still find the marks of wanton hunger on the faces of women and children, and like Sandburg, you can see the gunman kill and go free to kill again.

And yet, for every shudder of the Big Shoulders, there is a soft surprise—like the delicate watercolor pastels Visalli found when the May sun splashed its morning light across Oak Street Beach. And there is what Visalli calls the "tangible culture" that grows beneath the austere towers of steel and cement: the works of Picasso, Miró, Dubuffet, Calder, Chagall, and Henry Moore, not sheltered behind Gothic columns for a few but hugging the sidewalks for the people in the finest public-art gallery in the country.

It was inevitable that the faces of Chicago would change, too, as the neighborhoods shifted their character. Irish, Germans, Italians, and Poles stirred rich cultures into Chicago's melting pot. While you can still eat pierogis on Milwaukee Avenue without hearing English spoken, many of the Europeans who came to Packingtown for work, who laid the sewers and built the city, have seen their children move to suburbs. New immigrants have come to blend Hispanic and Asian faces with Chicago's black population. Now, the ethnic tapestry is even more colorful and more representative of the nations of the world.

A Cambodian woman proudly showed me a tiny urban garden she had scratched out of a vacant lot in Uptown. Her family had escaped the terrors of war by walking hundreds of miles to the safety of Thailand where they waited in refugee camps to be sent to America—and Chicago. She reached down to the growing plants and picked several tiny seeds. Then, in broken English, she explained how she had carried a few such seeds in her dress all the way from the other side of the world so she could plant them in her new home. No plants like these had ever grown in Chicago before, but they were thriving, even in the soil of a vacant lot still mixed with broken glass and splinters. Everything about her was different, except her story. Chicago has heard it millions of times in different ways as it goes on building, breaking, rebuilding, always making room for someone else to tell the story.

The Chicago revealed in these photographs will look different from any previously documented, but even her most futuristic structures are inescapably linked to a past when her citizens dreamed of rebuilding a city from ashes and had the temerity to plan "the greatest city in the world." The *new* Chicago documented by Santi Visalli is proof their dreams are still alive and growing.

BONWIT TELL

We struck the home-trail now, and in a few hours were in that astonishing Chicago—a city where they are always rubbing the lamp, and fetching up the genii, and contriving and achieving new impossibilities. It is hopeless for the occasional visitor to try to keep up with Chicago—she outgrows his prophecies faster than he can make them. She is always a novelty; for she is never the Chicago you saw when you passed the last time.

Mark Twain, 1883

On either side of the vista in converging lines stretched
the blazing office buildings. But over the end of the
street the lead-coloured sky was rifted a little. A long,
faint bar of light stretched across the prospect, and sil-
houetted against this rose a sombre mass, unbroken by
any lights, rearing a black and formidable facade
against the blur of light behind it ... the pile of the
Board of Trade Building, black, grave, monolithic,
crouching on its foundations, like a monstrous sphinx
with blind eyes, silent, grave—crouching there without a
sound, without a sign of life under the night and the
drifting veil of rain.

Frank Norris, 1902

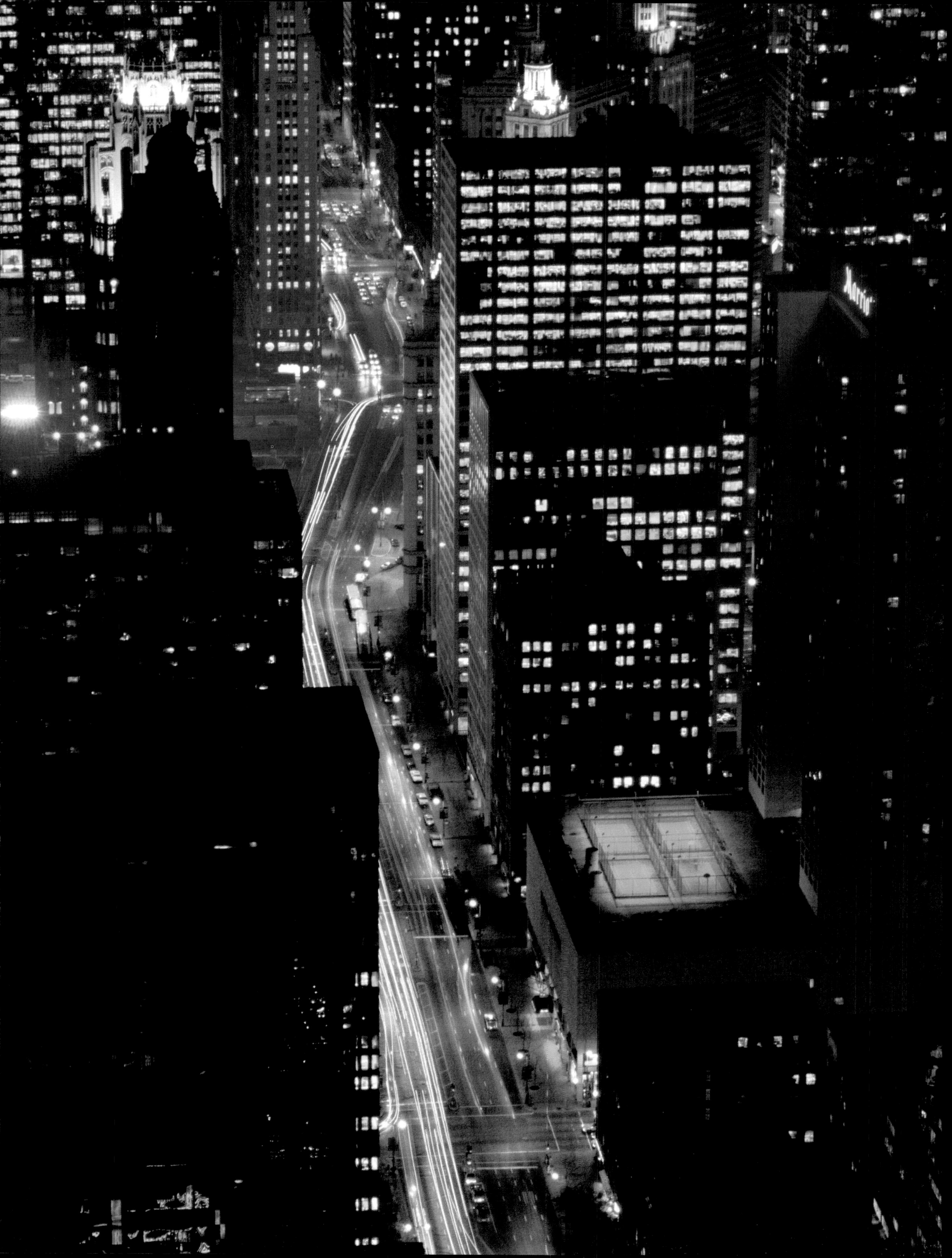

I am going away on the red, wild runaway moon.

Carl Sandburg

I AM THAT I AM

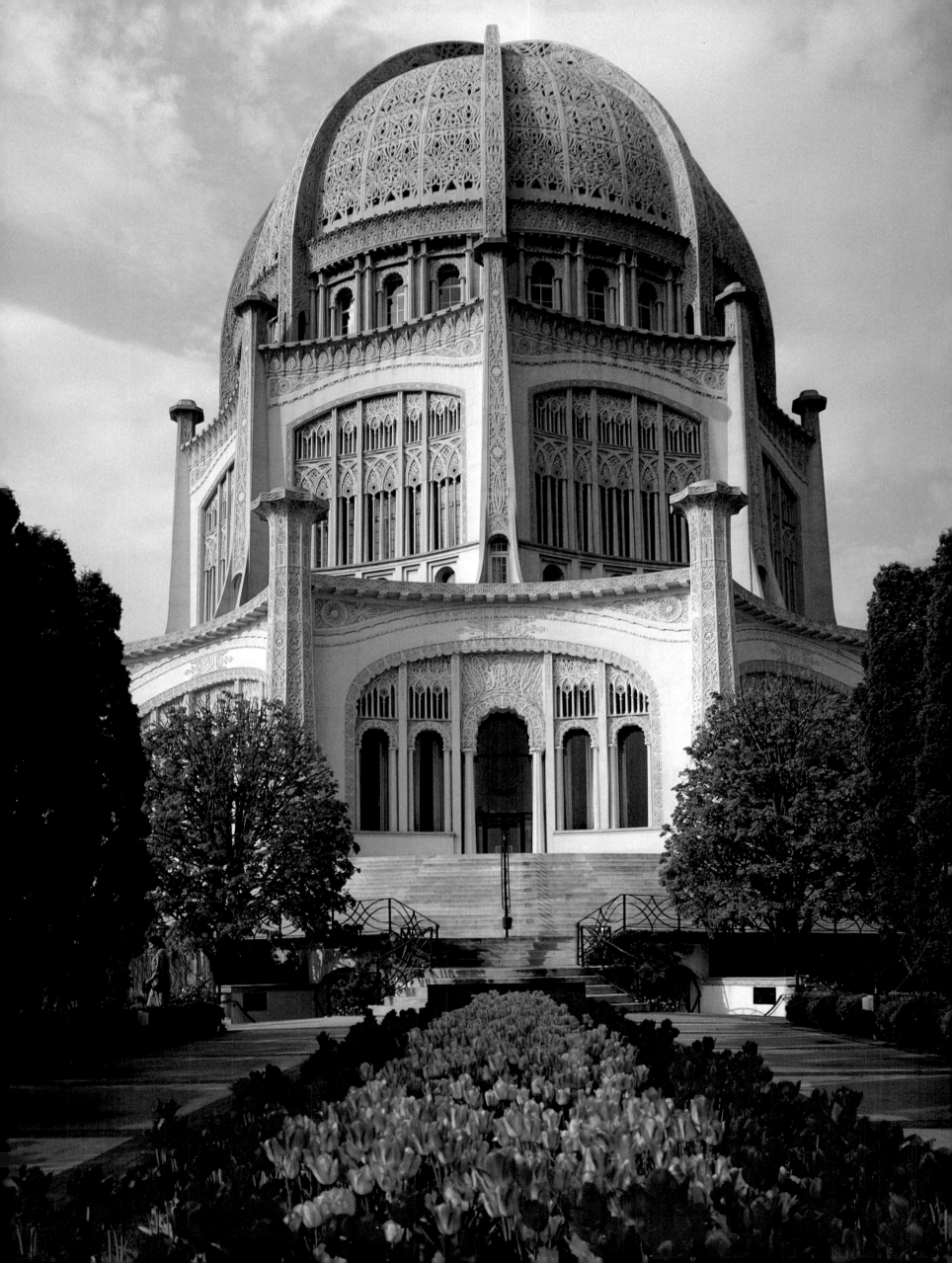

Janus, the two-faced god, has both blessed and cursed the city-state Chicago. Though his graven image is not visible to the naked eye, his ambiguous spirit soars atop Sears, Big Stan, and Big John. (Our city is street-wise and alley-hip of the casually familiar. Thus the Standard Oil Building and the John Hancock are, with tavern gaminess, referred to as Big Stan and Big John. Sears is simply that; never mind Roebuck. Ours is a one-syllable town. Its character has been molded by the muscle rather than the word.)

Studs Terkel

141

*With me, architecture is not an art, but a religion, and
that religion but a part of democracy.*

Louis H. Sullivan

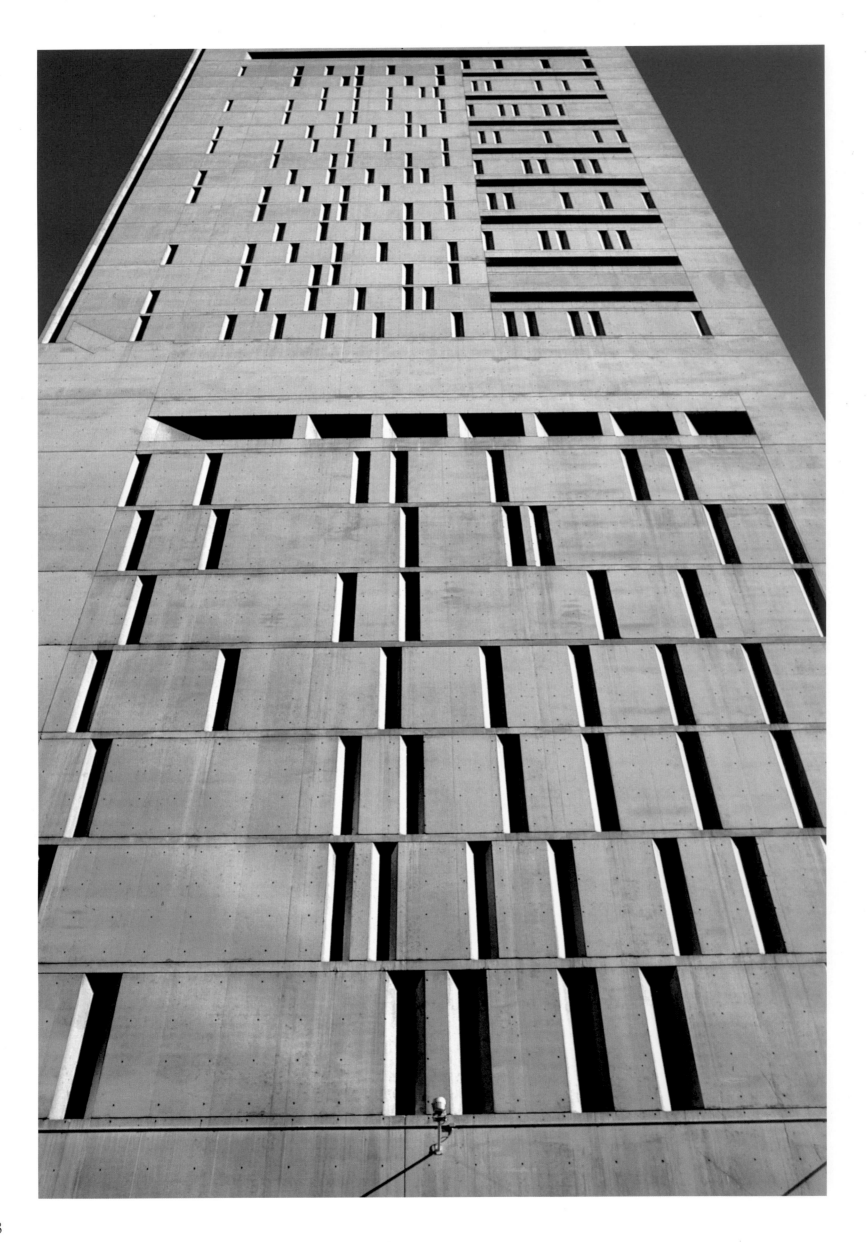

Dankmar Adler, builder and philosopher, together with his young partner, a genius rebel from the Beaux-Arts of Paris, Louis H. Sullivan, were practicing architecture there in Chicago about 1887. . . . I wanted to go to work for the great moderns, Adler and Sullivan, and finally I went.

Frank Lloyd Wright

YE'VE LEFT A GLIMMER STILL TO CHEER
THE MAN—THE ARTIFEX
THAT HOLDS IN SPITE O'KNOCKS AND SCALE
O'FRICTION WASTE AN' SLIP,
AN' BY THAT LIGHT—NOW MARK MY WORD—
WE'LL BUILD THE PERFECT SHIP.

167

By nights when the yellow salamanders of the El bend all one way and the cold rain runs with red-lit rain. By the way the city's million wires are burdened only by lightest snow; and the old year yet lighter upon them. When chairs are stacked and glasses are turned and arc-lamps all are dimmed. By days when the wind bangs alley gates ajar and the sun goes by on the wind. By nights when the moon is an only child above the measured thunder of the cars, you may know Chicago's heart at last.

Nelson Algren, 1951

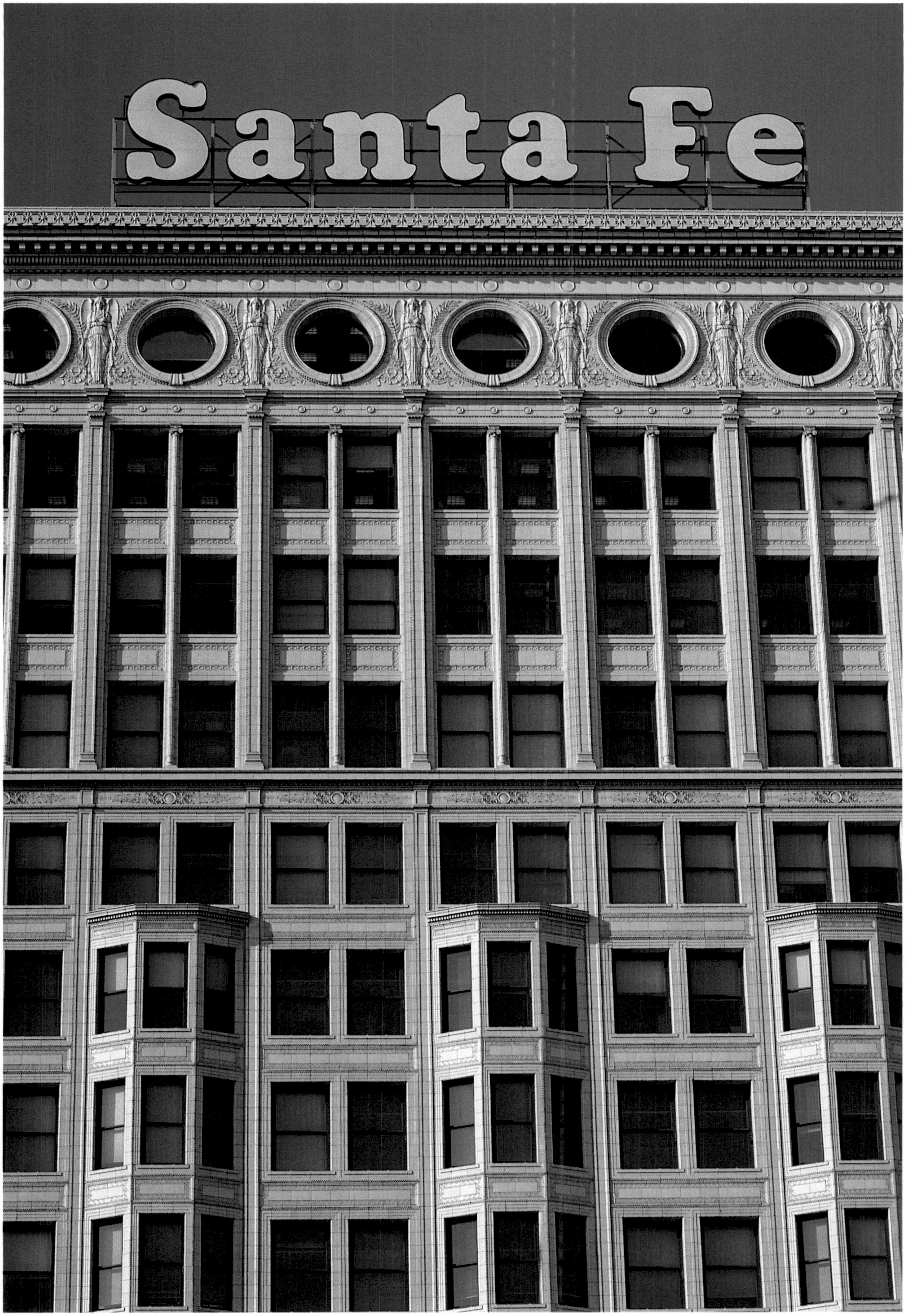
Santa Fe

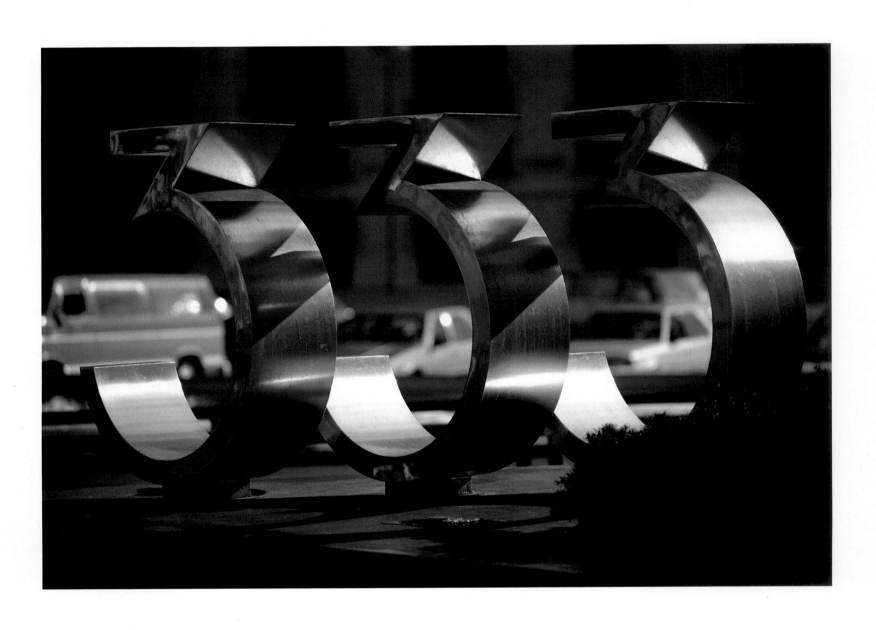

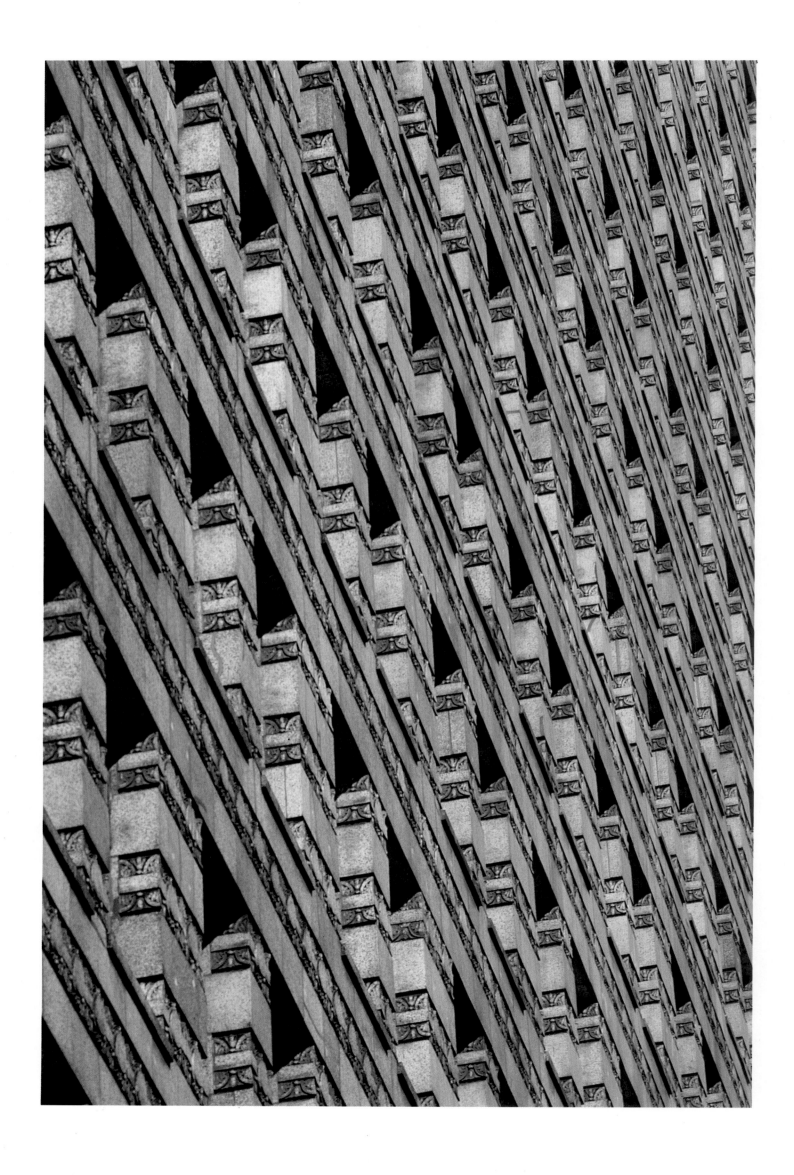

I adore Chicago. It is the pulse of America!

Sarah Bernhardt

Three of my friends were killed in the last two weeks in Chicago. That certainly is not conducive to peace of mind.

Al Capone, 1929

Nobody can think of Chicago as actually existing; a person would go mad if he did; it is a grotesque nightmare and easily recognizable as such.

Don Marquis, 1932

It is a champion of a city!

Mayor Harold Washington, 1986

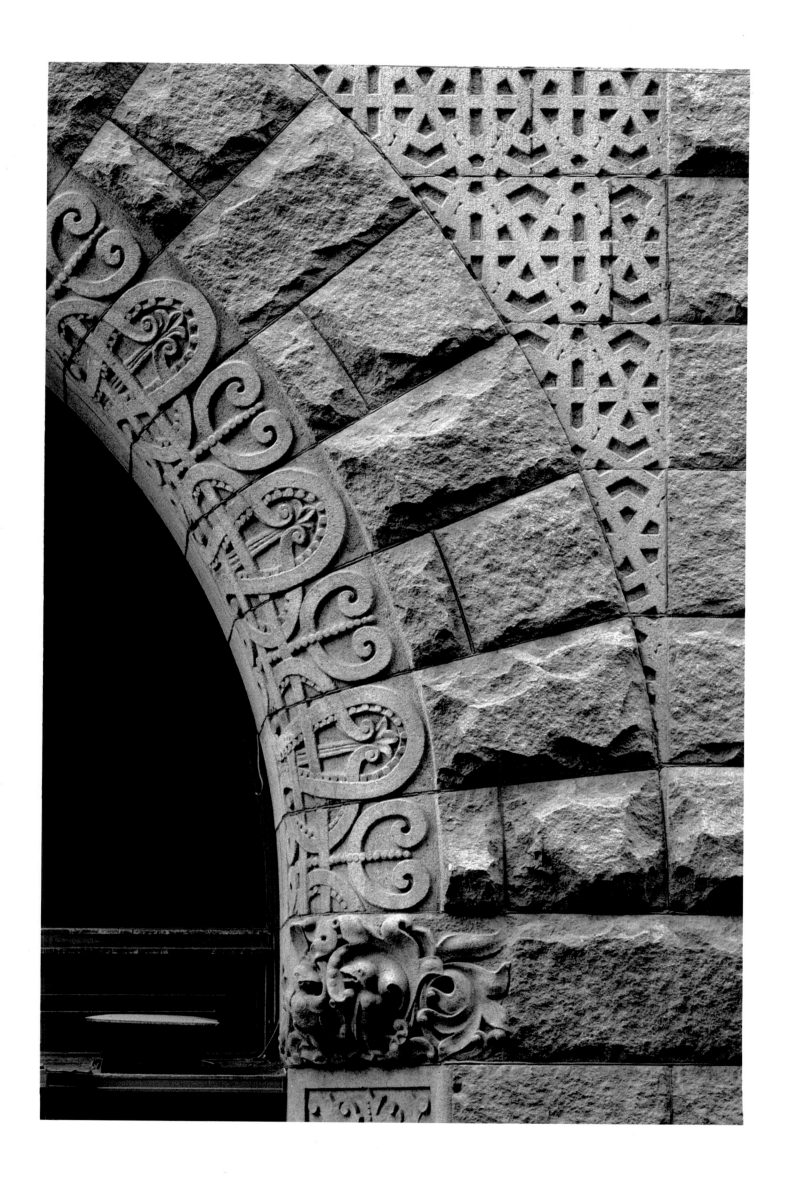

211

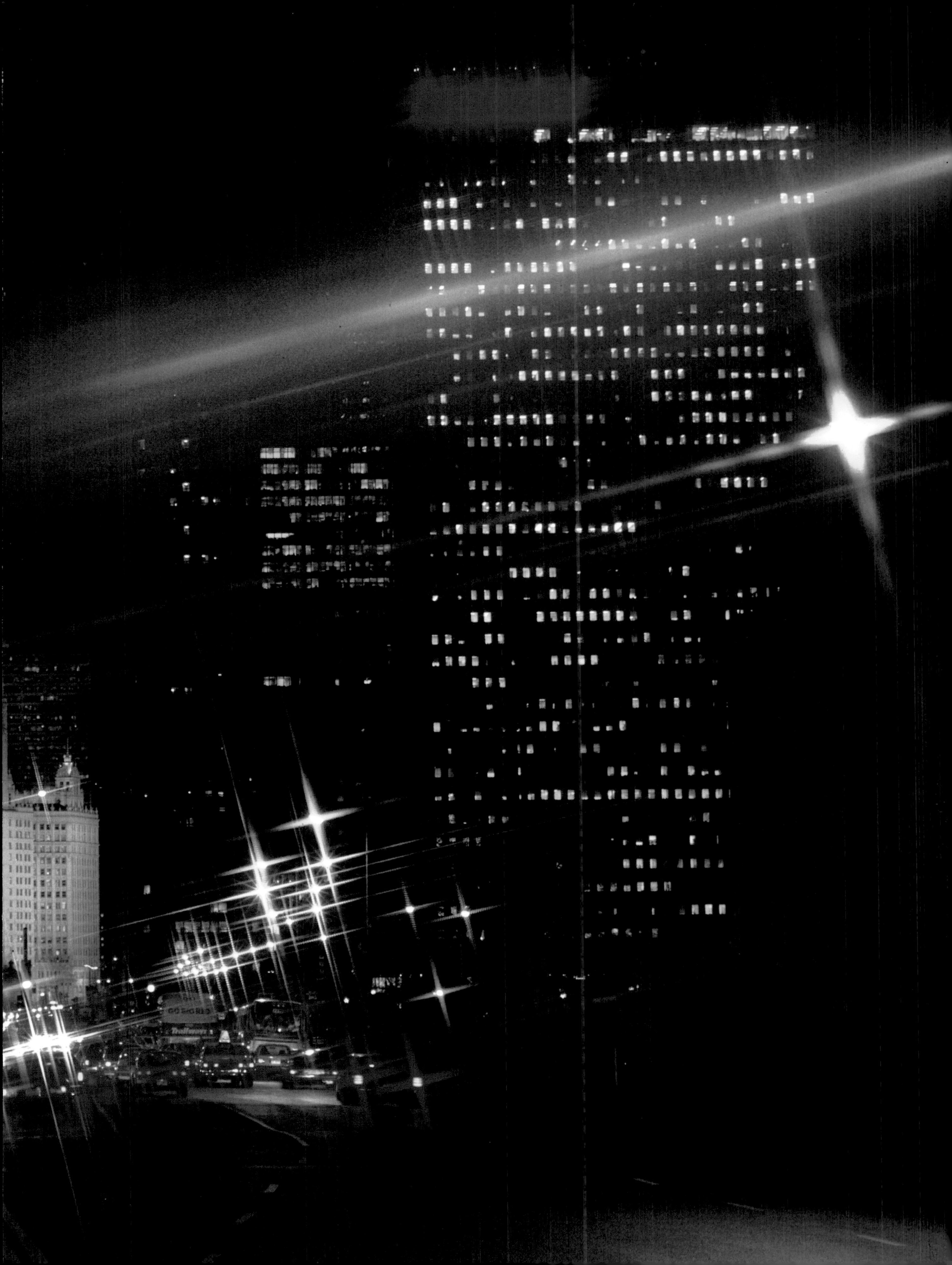

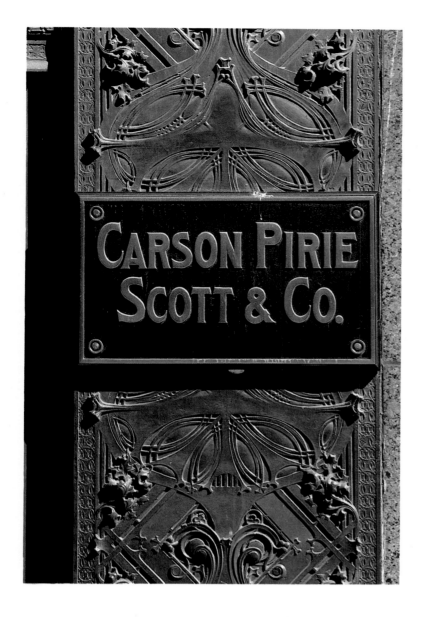

The country went broke in 1929. On the public lagoon, rowing, we read Keats to each other while the weeds bound the oars. Chicago was nowhere. It had no setting. It was something released into American space. It was where trains arrived; where mail orders were dispatched. But on the lagoon, with turning boats, the water and the sky clear green, pure blue, the boring power of a great manufacturing center arrested (there was no smoke, the mills were crippled—industrial distress benefited the atmosphere), Zet recited "Upon the honeyed middle of the night ..."

Saul Bellow

ILLUSTRATIONS

A date in parentheses indicates year of completion of a building or a work of art

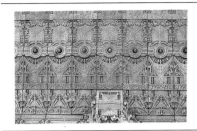

1: Detail of Krause Music Store facade (1922), designed by Louis H. Sullivan

2: In foreground, Clarence Buckingham Fountain (1927), Grant Park; in background, Sears Tower (1974), CNA Center (1972), McCormick Building (1910), and 310 South Michigan Avenue (1926)

13: Detail of The Rookery Building (1886), Burnham and Root, architects

15: View of skyline along South Michigan Avenue, with Sears Tower (1974), world's tallest building, in background

16–17: Chicago skyline, looking northeast from Sears Tower, 110th-floor rooftop, with Lake Michigan in background

18–19: Moon over Chicago, viewed from Max Adler Planetarium

20: 333 West Wacker Drive (1983), Kohn Pedersen Fox, architects

21: Chicago River on St. Patrick's Day; at right, Marina City (1964, 1967), Bertrand Goldberg Associates, architects

22–23: Dwight D. Eisenhower Expressway; upper right, U.S. Post Office

24–25: Skyward view of John Hancock Center (1969), Skidmore, Owings and Merrill, architects

26: Lake Point Tower (1968), Schipporeit-Heinrich Associates, architects; viewed from north

27: In foreground, top of 666 North Lake Shore Drive (1923), on McClurg Court; in background, facade of Onterie Center apartments (1986), at 441 East Erie Street

28–29: View of North Lake Shore Drive on rainy day

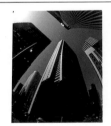

30: First National Bank Building (1969), C. F. Murphy Associates, architects

31: In foreground, slanted roof of Associates Center (1983), on Michigan Avenue

32–33: Presidential Towers apartments (1986)

35: Reception room of Elks National Memorial Building (1926), Egerton Swartwout, architect

48: Old bridge framing skyline over Chicago River, along Wacker Drive

36–37: Fashionable Gold Coast along North Lake Shore Drive, near Oak Street Beach

49: Sanitation Department snowman standing guard in front of untitled sculpture (1967), by Pablo Picasso, on Richard J. Daley Plaza

38: View of 247-foot antenna on top of Sears Tower

50–51: Ice floes on Chicago River; on north bank, Chicago Sun-Times (1957) and Wrigley (1921–24) buildings

39: View from Sears Tower, looking northeast; at right, Standard Oil Building (1974; also called Amoco Building), Chicago's second-tallest building, Edward Durell Stone, architect

52–53: Winter view; upper left, Lincoln Park, and right, North Street Beach

40–41: View of Max Adler Planetarium (1930; Ernest A. Grunsfeld, architect) on cold November day

55: Night view of Magnificent Mile, looking south

42–43: Bronze sculpture *Nuclear Energy* (1967), by Henry Moore, University of Chicago, commemorating first nuclear chain reaction on December 2, 1942, achieved by Enrico Fermi and his associates

56–57: Lobby of Palmer House (1925)

44: Reflection of Chicago in a Salvation Army horn

58: CNA Center (1972), 325 South Wabash Avenue, Graham, Anderson, Probst and White, architects

45: Skyward view of Associates Center

59: Gargoyle, University of Chicago

46–47: Painted-steel sculpture *Flamingo* (1974), by Alexander Calder, 53 feet high, on Federal Plaza at Dearborn and Adams streets

60–61: Window washer, People's Gas, Light and Coke Co. Building (1910), 122 South Michigan Avenue

62: Krause Music Store facade (1922), designed by Louis H. Sullivan

72–73: Boating on Chicago River

63: Carson Pirie Scott & Co. (1899, 1903–04), Louis H. Sullivan, architect

74–75: Mural in Pilsen, 16th Street and Blue Island

64–65: Trading hours, Chicago Board of Trade (1930), 141 West Jackson Boulevard

77: Moonlight over Drake Tower

66: Standard Oil Building seen through bronze sculpture *Large Interior Form* (1983), by Henry Moore, The Art Institute of Chicago

78–79: John G. Shedd Aquarium (1929), Graham, Anderson, Probst and White, architects

67: Standard Oil Building seen from Richard J. Daley Plaza

80: View from Lake Michigan of the Associates Center (1983), far left; Prudential Building (1955), center; and Standard Oil Building (1974), far right

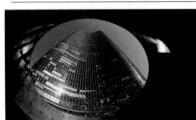

68–69: Lake Point Tower

81: Sears Tower (1974) at sunrise

70: Top, horse and carriage on Michigan Avenue, Christmas Day, 1986

82–83: Night view of skyline from North Street Beach; tallest building, John Hancock Center

70: Bottom, chestnut vendor in front of Marshall Field's, Christmas Day, 1986

84–85: Bronze *Sundial* (1980), by Henry Moore, in front of Max Adler Planetarium

71: Colonnade of Union Station (1917), designed by Graham, Burnham and Company

86: *American Gothic* (1930), by Grant Wood, The Art Institute of Chicago

87: Gerald Johns, Chicago Tourism Council guide, Water Tower Pumping Station

101: Marshall's Field's Walnut Room, Christmas 1986. The tree, 45 feet tall and decorated with 5,000 handmade ornaments, stands in court designed by D. H. Burnham and Company

88–89: Mosaic mural *The Four Seasons* (1974), by Marc Chagall, 10 feet high by 70 feet long, on First National Plaza, Dearborn and Monroe streets

102: Chicago Theater (1921), 175 North State Street, C. W. and George L. Rapp, architects

90: Entrance to Railway Exchange Building (1904), D. H. Burnham and Company, architects

103: Baha'i House of Worship (1920–53), Wilmette, Illinois

91: Museum of Science and Industry, Rosenwald Court (founded 1932). The Museum occupies the Palace of Fine Arts built for World's Columbian Exposition (1893)

104–05: Facade of Manhattan Building (1890), 431 South Dearborn Street, William LeBaron Jenney, architect

92–93: Night view of Spaghetti Junction, interchange of Dwight D. Eisenhower, John F. Kennedy, and Dan Ryan expressways

106–07: Detail of facade, Marina City apartment buildings

94: O'Hare Rapid Transit Station (1983), Helmut Jahn, architect

108: In foreground, steel sculpture *Batcolumn* (1977), by Claes Oldenburg, 100 feet high, at 600 West Madison Street

95: O'Hare Rapid Transit Station

109: *Alexander Hamilton* (1952), by John Angel, Lincoln Park Plaza

96–97: Victory day at Wrigley Field: Chicago Cubs defeat the Atlanta Braves

110–11: Sir Georg Solti conducting rehearsal of Chicago Symphony Orchestra at Orchestra Hall

98–99: University of Chicago campus

112–13: South facade of The Art Institute of Chicago (1892), Shepley, Rutan and Coolidge, architects

114: Chicago Board of Trade (1930), Holabird and Root, architects

122–23: Skating in Richard J. Daley Bicentennial Plaza, December 1986, with skyline and South Michigan Avenue in background

115: Top left, C. D. Peacock jewelry store, Palmer House (1925)

124–25: Interior of State of Illinois Center (1985), Helmut Jahn, architect

115: Top right, 35 East Wacker Drive (1926)

126: Top, floor of State of Illinois Center

115: Bottom left, American National Bank (1928)

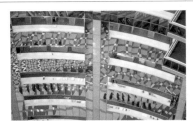

126: Bottom, detail of State of Illinois Center

115: Bottom right, Marshall Field's (1907)

127: Exterior of State of Illinois Center; in foreground, fiberglass sculpture *Monument with Standing Beast* (1984), by Jean Dubuffet, 29 feet high

116–17: Night view from John Hancock Center, looking south

128: Terra-cotta pharaoh on facade of Reebie Storage and Moving Co. (1923), North Clark Street

118: Reflections on building near Van Buren Street

129: Trompe-l'oeil painting (1984), by Richard Haas, on Reliable Corporation building, 1001 Van Buren Street

119: 860–80 Lake Shore Drive apartments (1952), Ludwig Mies van der Rohe, architect

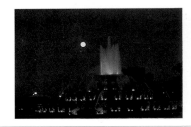

130–31: Moonrise over Buckingham Fountain, Grant Park

121: View of skyline with low clouds cutting off all but the tops of tall buildings

132–33: Bird's-eye view of city from Max Adler Planetarium

 134: Chicago River between 35 East Wacker Drive (1926), left, and Marina City (1964, 1967) right

 148: Detail of Getty Tomb (1890), Graceland Cemetery, designed by Louis H. Sullivan

 135: Busts in front of Merchandise Mart honoring eight leading American businessmen

 149: Top left, trompe-l'oeil painting *Homage to the Chicago School of Architecture* (1980), by Richard Haas, 1211 North LaSalle Street; from left, Frank Lloyd Wright, John W. Root, Daniel Burnham, and Louis H. Sullivan

 136–37: Pagoda of On Leong Chinese Merchants Association (1930), Michaelson and Rognstad, architects

 149: Top right, fanlight of 120 Cedar Street

 138–39: Rush-hour traffic on Columbus Drive, looking north

 149: Bottom left, detail of Glessner house (1886), 1800 South Prairie Avenue, H. H. Richardson, architect

 140: Mayfair Regent Hotel

 149: Bottom right, fanlight of 60 Cedar Street

 141: 60 Cedar Street

 150: *The Bowman and the Spearman* (1928), by Ivan Mestrovic, Grant Park

 142–43: Oak Street Beach and North Lake Shore Drive

 151: In foreground, *Theodore Thomas Memorial* (1923), by Albin Polasek, tribute to founder of Chicago Symphony Orchestra, Grant Park; lower left, Orchestra Hall

 144–45: Auditorium Theater (1889), Adler and Sullivan, architects

 152–53: Trading hours, Chicago Mercantile Exchange

 147: Christmas decorations at Water Tower Place (1976; Loebl, Schlossman, Bennett and Dart, architects, and Warren Platner, interior)

 154–55: Faces nightclub, North Rush Street

156: Interior of *Monument with Standing Beast* (1984), by Jean Dubuffet, State of Illinois Center

167: *Lion* (1894), by Edward Kemeys, The Art Institute of Chicago

157: Merchandise Mart (1930) viewed from LaSalle Street Bridge

168–69: A. Finkl & Sons, steel-forging company, established 1879

158: Facade of Metropolitan Correctional Center (1975), Harry Weese and Associates, architects

170: Ornamental detail over main entrance to Oriental Theater, State Street

159: Facade of Metropolitan Correctional Center

171: Ivy-covered town house

160–61: Detail of Standard Oil Building

172–73: Interior of Chicago Theater

162: Fire escape on North Clark Street

174: African elephants, Great Hall, Field Museum of Natural History

163: *Chicago Sun-Times* delivery man

175: Giraffes, Lincoln Park Zoo

165: Frank Lloyd Wright studio (ca. 1900), Oak Park, Illinois

176: Buckingham Fountain, Grant Park

166: Garden wedding at Patterson-McCormick Mansion (1892), designed by Stanford White

177: New Year celebration in Chinatown

178–79: Dawn over Lake Michigan

190: Pine-Top Perkins playing blues at Rosa's, West Armitage Street

180: Murals and trompe-l'oeil painting in Pilsen, Mexican neighborhood

191: Lyric Opera of Chicago on opening night of production *Un Ballo in Maschera,* 1986

181: Trompe-l'oeil painting in Pilsen

192: Auditorium Theater

183: North Lake Shore Drive at night

193: Top, Chicago Theater

184: North Lake Shore Drive during rush hour

193: Bottom, Patterson-McCormick Mansion

185: Facade and cornice of Railway Exchange Building, South Michigan Avenue

194–95: Foreground, sculpture *Being Born* (1983), by Virginio Ferrari, on Washington Street

186: Detail of 79 Cedar Street

196: Sculptured numerals of 333 West Wacker Drive

187: Town house, 1352 LaSalle Street

197: Detail of Heald Fountain, Heald Square

188–89: Railroad right of way on West Side

198–99: Skyline, looking northeast from 110th floor of Sears Tower

200: Detail of facade, People's Gas, Light and Coke Co. (1910), 122 South Michigan Avenue

211: Detail of The Rookery Building

201: Detail of facade, 435 North Michigan Avenue

212–13: After trading hours at Midwest Stock Exchange

203: Atrium of Three First National Building

214: William W. Kimball Mansion

204: Garden of The Art Institute of Chicago

215: Town house, Astor Street

205: Top, Al Capone's grave, Mount Carmel Cemetery

216: C. D. Peacock jewelry store, Palmer House

205: Bottom, Louis H. Sullivan's grave, Graceland Cemetery

217: Christmas lights on the Magnificent Mile, 1986

206–07: Belmont Harbor

218–19: South Michigan Avenue at night, with Wrigley Building in center

208–09: Skyline, looking west from Max Adler Planetarium

220: Chicago Tribune Tower (1925), Hood and Howells, architects

210: Detail of The Rookery Building (1886), Burnham and Root, architects

221: Carbide and Carbon Building (1929), 230 North Michigan Avenue, Burnham Brothers, architects

222: Detail of door, James Charnley house (1892), 1365 North Astor Street, designed by Frank Lloyd Wright when at Adler and Sullivan, architects; now owned by Skidmore Owings and Merrill Foundation

228–29: A 23-below-zero November morning on Lake Michigan

223: Top left, Carson Pirie Scott & Co., ornament by Louis H. Sullivan

230–31: Sunrise over Lake Michigan

223: Top right, Carson Pirie Scott & Co., ornament by Louis H. Sullivan

232: Town house on Elm Street

223: Bottom left, Carson Pirie Scott & Co., ornament by Louis H. Sullivan

233: New Michigan Hotel, on South Side, formerly Al Capone's headquarters

223: Bottom right, detail of elevator grillwork from Stock Exchange Building (1894–96; demolished), designed by Louis H. Sullivan; now owned by Chicago Historical Society

234–35: View of downtown, looking east toward Loop

224–25: Lobby of Drake Hotel (1920), Marshall and Fox, architects

236–37: Early morning fog

227: General Grant and paddleboat rider, Lincoln Park